LIVING DANGEROUSLY

STUNT PERFORMERS

DEREK WARE

GEC GARRETT EDUCATIONAL CORPORATION

LIVING **DANGEROUSLY**

ASTRONAUTS
DIVERS
FIREFIGHTERS

PILOTS
RACING DRIVERS
STUNT PERFORMERS

Series Editor: James Kerr
Designers: Helen White, Jackie Berry

Cover: Stunt performers from *Miami Vice* execute
a stunt with explosives.

Edited by Rebecca Stefoff

© 1992 by Garrett Educational Corporation
First published in the United States in 1992 by
Garrett Educational Corporation
130 East 13th Street, Ada, OK 74820

© 1991 Wayland Publishers, Limited
First published in 1991 by Wayland
Publishers, Limited

Printed in Italy. Bound in USA.

Library of Congress Cataloging in Publication Data

Ware, Derek, 1938-
    Stunt performers/Derek Ware.
        p. cm.—(Living dangerously)
    Includes index.
    Summary: Describes the skill and training needed
by professional stunt performers and the dangers
they face as a part of their work.
    ISBN 1-56074-045-0
    1. Stunt men and women—Juvenile literature.
[1. Stunt men and women.]
I. Title. II. Series.
PN1995.9.S7W37   1992
91.43'028'0922—dc20
                                        91-41209
                                          CIP
                                          AC

CONTENTS

BUMP GUYS 4

FALL GIRLS...8

FALLS AND FIRE 12

RIDING RISKS...17

CAR CHASES, CRASHES, AND
CATASTROPHES....................................21

SPIELBERG'S STUNTS – INDIANA
JONES..26

GLOSSARY 30

INDEX..32

BUMP *GUYS*

Performing stunts for films and TV probably sounds like exciting work. Just think of crashing a flaming car like those in *Days of Thunder*, flying a jet plane through a series of aerobatics as in *Top Gun*, or charging through cannon fire and explosions similar to those in *Glory*. Imagine clashing broadswords for films like *Highlander*, *The Princess Bride*, and *Robin Hood*. What about falling through windows, tumbling down stairs, and toppling off balconies for comedy movies such as *Home Alone*, *The Goonies*, and the *Police Academy* series? Performing these stunts would seem to be an exciting way to make a living. But have you thought what being a professional stunt performer really means?

Sometimes stars do their own stunts – Timothy Dalton in *License to Kill*.

Arnold Schwarzenegger's muscles help him out of a tight spot in *Total Recall*.

Performing stunts, or stunting, is not a job for daredevils. The people who make a career out of stunting never take a chance. The actions they perform are not the result of being challenged to do something "for a dare." They will not attempt any stunt that has not been carefully planned to the smallest detail. This book will show what qualities stunt performers need to begin with, and what skills they must acquire to be successful.

A stunt is based on the principle of illusion, like the work of a stage magician whose tricks appear to be the result of magic. A magic trick is achieved by the magician's "sleight of hand," while a stunt is achieved by the performer's know-how. Both make us see what they want us to see. This skill is not something that can be gained overnight. Anyone can take a chance and do something dangerous once.

A stunt performer may have to do a dangerous action three or four times before the film's director is satisfied he or she has got the best "take."

Seventy-five years ago there were no stunt performers. If a scene in a film called for a character to tumble down stairs, whoever was playing the part was expected to do it. Later, when the film companies started substituting doubles for the actors, they didn't call them stunt performers but "special action extras," "danger personnel," or "bump guys."

Harold Lloyd, one of the first great stunt stars. He worked entirely without a double on the 1923 movie *Safety Last*.

Modern day "danger personnel" stunting on *Back to the Future II*.

Stunting in those days was a profession with no veterans because nobody had done it before. Film companies had to hire bump guys from elsewhere. They used circus acrobats, ex-clowns, and knock-about comedians from the music hall and vaudeville theaters. To re-create a medieval battle successfully required horsemen willing to ride in full armor with swords and shields. No ordinary person had done this for more than 300 years. Comedy films and thrillers needed drivers who could handle motor vehicles at top speeds, at a time when most people didn't own a car and couldn't drive. These pioneer movie "extras" were daring people who paved the way for modern stunt performers, who know there's more to stunting nowadays than just going bump. . . .

The first stunt woman was Jean de Kay who, for a film entitled *Our Mutual Girl*, had to be knocked over by a car. The *New York Times* reported in 1915: ". . . Miss de Kay jumped into the air as she was struck and landed full on the mudguard, thus avoiding going under the wheels. . . ."

A modern stunt woman would never allow herself to be struck by a car. She would carry a number of articles such as an umbrella, a handbag and gloves, or a shopping basket. She would flip these into the air at the moment of the car's apparent impact. By doing this she would direct the audience's eyes away for a moment. She would then perform a somersault, allowing the car to miss her.

An example of early stunting – the stunt woman is just going to have to jump and hope for the best. . . .

There is no limit to the type of stunts women can attempt. In Hollywood in the 1930s and 1940s, Betty Danko specialized in falls. She once fell 30 feet (9 meters) into a shallow tank of water. Audrey Scott rode on horseback and drove wagons and stagecoaches for 45 years. Mary Wiggens could fly planes, walk on airplane wings, and parachute. She once crashed two locomotives head on, escaping with a broken thumb. In recent times, Jennie Epper has been scooped up by a bulldozer and dumped into a rubbish truck for the film *Soylent Green*. For *Earthquake* she had to appear to be crushed by a falling elevator.

One of the first female stunt performers – Helen Gibson – as she appeared in *The Hazards of Helen*.

Nevertheless, women are at a disadvantage when performing certain stunts. When working with fire, for instance, there is a danger that their hair may ignite because of the lacquer and sprays they may have to wear. When they take any kind of fall, stunt performers wear body padding, most notably on the knees and elbows. Stunt men, usually dressed in jackets, shirts, and trousers, are able to cover these pads. If stunt women are wearing skirts and blouses, they are often unable to "pad up" at all. Some have other problems to deal with. The American stunt woman Kitty O'Neil, who is part Cherokee, has been deaf since the age of five. This didn't stop her from becoming a stunt performer doubling for Linda Carter in the *Wonder Woman* series on TV. She holds numerous land and water speed records and appears in *The Guinness Book of Records* as holder of the highest fall performed by a woman, 177 feet (54 meters). Once the cameras are rolling the only way the director can give her the signal for "action" — since she cannot hear — is to fire a pistol, from which she picks up the shock waves.

An obvious male double takes a dive for the actress Barbara Hershey in *The Stunt Man*. Union rules now require stunt women to double for actresses.

A stunt woman attempts a tricky car-to-car transfer in *Footloose*.

Danger Fact

For the film *Annie* nine-year-old Aileen Quinn had to appear to transfer from a twenty-story drawbridge to a helicopter. Actually, it was thirty-seven-year-old Bobby Porter dressed in identical clothes. At 4'7" (1.4 meters) tall, he is the smallest stunt performer in the business.

As there are no stunt children in films, the job of doubling for young people usually falls to stunt women. Some stunt performers started their careers at an early age. British stunter Connie Tilton started at the age of thirteen. Loretta Rush, a high school diving champion, was sixteen when she did her first stunt – a dive off a cliff into a stone quarry. More recently, nineteen-year-old Debbie Evans, junior motorcycling champion, rode bikes on *Death Sport* and the *CHIPS* TV series. She has since gone on to make a career for herself in films like *The Jerk*, which starred Steve Martin, *1941*, and *Airplane*.

FALLS AND FIRE

Certainly one of the most spectacular feats of the stunt performer is the high fall. Over the years the heights stunt men and women have fallen from have amazed movie audiences. In the 1950s, 43 feet (13 meters) was considered the limit. Thirty years later the record stood at a staggering 234 feet (71 meters). What has assisted these remarkable advances has been the development of the high fall rig, or "catcher." This is the apparatus used to break or cushion the stunter's fall.

Stunt performers, handcuffed together, execute a high fall for _Lethal Weapon_.

A box rig set up for a vertical fall in *Indiana Jones and the Temple of Doom*.

In the early days falls of up to 16 feet (5 meters) were taken onto ordinary mattresses. For anything higher, a trapeze artist's net was required. By 1930 the box rig had been devised. This was a collection of empty cardboard boxes stacked on top of each other. In the 1960s the box rig was mounted on wooden planks resting on the inflated inner tubes of car tires. This enabled the stunt performer to take higher falls. A later innovation was the crash pad – a canvas rectangle filled with foam rubber, similar to those used by pole-vaulters. When set up on a sprung box rig, it allowed still higher falls. Finally came the air bag, made of lightweight plastic and inflated with warm air.

The 1970s saw the first use of the descender wire, which allows stunt artists to drop from great heights. It has been used on many films, including *Escape to Athena*, which starred Roger Moore, *Green Ice*, *Supergirl*, and the *Superman* series. Stunter Dar Robinson used it to enable him to make a leap from the 117-story CN Tower in Toronto, Canada. For the 1980 film *Highpoint*, at the same location, he repeated the stunt – with a variation. The difference was that he didn't use a descender wire or any form of rig on the ground, which was 1,170 feet (356.6 meters) below! "How can he possibly survive?" was the thought in the minds of the crowd looking up as he hurled himself into space. Six seconds later many of the people below were convinced that he wouldn't survive. They began to scatter, then stopped transfixed as, at 897 feet (273.3 meters), a parachute that had been concealed in his hip pocket opened out and enabled him to float the remaining 273 feet (83.3 meters) in complete safety.

Stunt performers, coordinators, and special effects personnel work as a team for scenes requiring the use of fire or explosives. For a fire sequence, the special effects unit provides an inflammable mixture that is smeared on the clothing of the stunt performer who is to be set on fire. The special effects crew are also responsible for igniting, controlling, and extinguishing all flames on or surrounding the stunt performer.

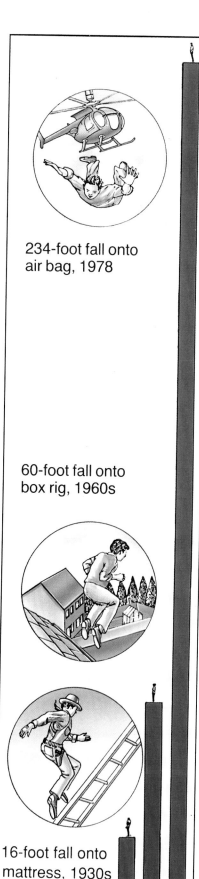

234-foot fall onto air bag, 1978

60-foot fall onto box rig, 1960s

16-foot fall onto mattress, 1930s

LEFT **Falls have gotten higher and higher since the early days of stunting.**

The simplest way of doing an explosives sequence is to have the stunt performer bounce off a trampoline as the special effects crew detonate the "flash powder" or "fireball." The stunt performer appears to be thrown through the air by the force of the blast. Another method is to use the air ram, a hinged board with a strong spring in the center. This is doubled over and held with a catch that is attached to an air cylinder. As the stunt performer steps on the board, a jet of compressed air releases the catch and throws him or her backward or forward. A third option is to use the jerk harness, which works like the descender wire but takes the stunt performer upward rather than downward. The grandfather character in the movie *National Lampoon's Christmas Vacation* appears to be blown up by this effect.

RIGHT **Stunter Chuck Bail leaps from one roof to another in *The Stunt Man*.**

Danger Fact

The highest free fall by a stunt performer in a film was by A. J. Bakunas for *Hooper* in 1978. Later, for a film called *Steel*, he attempted a fall of 315 feet (96 meters). He died when the air bag he had designed himself split on impact.

RIDING **RISKS**

LEFT A "full burn" fire stunt for *The Dead Pool*.

BELOW An example of the banned trip wire method of making a horse fall over, from the 1939 movie *Stagecoach*.

Most stunt performers agree that working with horses is potentially the most dangerous type of stunt work there is. The horse is an extremely unpredictable animal. American stunt performers, with their long tradition of Western films, must take credit for most of the classic stunt sequences with horses. Many of the stunt riders in silent films had actually been cowboys during the closing era of the Wild West. One of the best stunt riders was Yakima Canutt, an ex-rodeo star who was All-round Champion Cowboy five years running before going to Hollywood as a cowboy actor. When it was discovered that his voice was unsuitable for talking pictures, Canutt switched to stunt riding and stayed on in Hollywood doing stunts for the next twenty years. He became the acknowledged expert on stunts requiring horses to rear, fall, or jump off cliffs into water.

"Yak" also drove burning and exploding wagons, overturned carriages, and allowed himself to be dragged between the hooves of galloping stagecoach teams. He gave up stunt work to become one of the most successful second unit directors in the industry. His greatest achievement was the chariot race sequence in the 1959 version of *Ben Hur*. In 1967 he received a special Academy Award for a lifetime of service in motion pictures – the only stunt performer ever to be honored in this way.

Canutt's techniques and the safety equipment he created are in use today and can be seen in films like *Conan the Barbarian*, *Young Guns II*, *Back to the Future III*, and *Dances with Wolves*. Stunt riding sequences in these films involve the use of the "L" stirrup. This is a device invented by Canutt that ensures that a rider taking a saddle fall will not get a foot caught and be dragged by the galloping horse. Also used is the drag leather – a long strap with a quick release that the rider hangs onto when a stunt calls for him or her to

A stunt rider taking an over-the-shoulder fall. Note the elbow pads.

Handle to help rider transfer to stagecoach

Camera car and crew

"L" stirrup

A stunt rider transfers from horse to stagecoach.

appear to be dragged. Canutt also devised the somersault jacket, which is a vest with a hook between the shoulder blades. A wire is attached to the hook in order to assist the stunt rider to flip backward over the horse's rear.

Canutt was an expert at training horses to fall on command. In the first few decades of movies, horses were made to fall with the aid of trip wires fixed to their front legs. The wires were attached to wooden posts driven into the ground and the horse was forced into a canter with the wires running out behind it. When the lengths of wire reached their limit, the horse's legs would be snatched out from under it. The horse would stumble forward, turning completely over – if it was lucky!

This practice was cruel and unnecessary and has since been banned. Now, all falling horses are trained and can only carry out their action under the supervision of a member of an animal protection association. Further regulations ensure the safe treatment of horses on film sets at all times. For locations where the weather is extremely hot or severely cold, double horses are required for the principal horses. All horses are permitted to work only a certain number of hours a day – in fact, fewer hours than the actors or stunt performers who have to ride them. As one veteran stunt performer said: "For the amount of hours they work and the money they're paid – I'd be a horse in pictures any day!"

Harrison Ford attempts some hard riding in *Indiana Jones and the Last Crusade*. Note the "L" stirrup.

CAR CHASES, CRASHES, AND CATASTROPHES

A ramp jump. The sloping platform used to launch the car is hidden by the passing train.

Veteran stunt driver Cary Loftin is on record as saying: "It seems every picture today has something involving cars – thank God!" In a career spanning fifty-five years – he started in 1936 and his latest film is *The Rookie* – he has continued to perform death-defying sequences with cars. In 1969 he was given the task of staging a driving sequence for a thriller called *Bullitt* starring Steve McQueen. The result was a twelve-minute car chase that has since become a classic and has paved the way for car stunts that would have seemed impossible when Loftin began crashing cars all those years ago.

Since the 1960s driving specialists have been encouraged to let their imaginations soar. This has enabled the cars in films to fly – both literally, in *The Man with the Golden Gun*, and in fantasy, for *Chitty Chitty Bang Bang* and *The Love Bug*. Cars have also been driven underwater (*The Spy Who Loved Me*), transported upside-down one on top of the other (*The Electric Horseman* starring Robert Redford), and balanced on two wheels to drive through an alley (*Diamonds Are Forever*). Thanks to stunt performers, movie-goers have also seen cars totally demolished by crashing head-on into a pair of stationary bulldozers (*Vanishing Point*), seemingly demolished but still going (*A View to a Kill*), and leaping over numerous other vehicles (*Smokey & the Bandit*).

The start of a car roll at high speed.

A controlled "fireball" explosion for the film *Batman*.

The car's reputation for defying the laws of gravity in films was established by Thomas Chatterton. For *The Secret of the Submarine* made in 1916, he jumped a 35-foot (10.5-meter) gap left by a washed-out bridge. This distance has been bettered in numerous films since: the current record of 156 feet (47.7 meters) was set during *Smokey & the Bandit II* in 1981 by Gary Davis. Special mention should be made of the 360° spiral jump performed by "Bumps" Willard for *The Man with the Golden Gun* in 1974. Willard calculated the speed and distance of the jump on the NASA computer at Cornell University.

Whether it's a simple racing broadside stunt or an explosives-assisted rollover sequence, the preparation for a car crash is complex, with nothing left to chance. All internal fixtures in the car are removed. A piece of curved scaffolding called a rollbar is fitted vertically behind the driving seat. This prevents the roof from caving in and crushing the driver. The tank is filled with just enough fuel for the driver to perform the stunt. This is to minimize the possibility of fire on impact. In addition to body padding, the driver wears fireproof overalls, a crash helmet, and a surgical collar around the neck to prevent whiplash. Finally, the driver

Explosives are placed in various parts of the car in an explosives sequence.

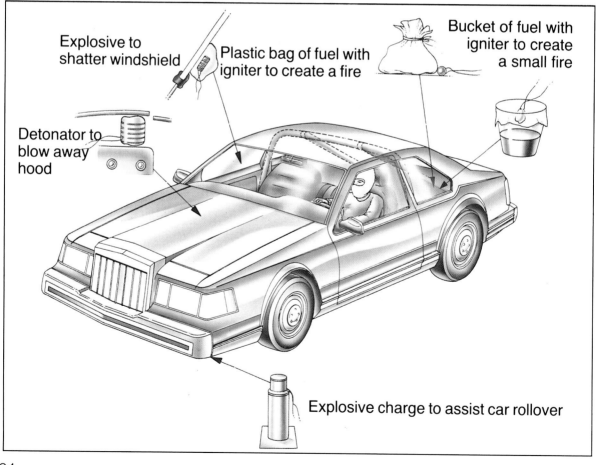

Explosive to shatter windshield

Plastic bag of fuel with igniter to create a fire

Bucket of fuel with igniter to create a small fire

Detonator to blow away hood

Explosive charge to assist car rollover

A motorcyclist takes a header over a car in *Hooper*. Trailing wires stop the bike from following the stunt performer.

is strapped into a racing driver's safety-harness with a quick release catch.

For a stunt such as taking a car off a pier into water, the same safety procedures are followed. Instead of flameproof clothing, a wet suit and diver's oxygen apparatus are worn. A hammer is carried on a strap around the wrist, to shatter the windshield once the car and driver are underwater. The stunt performer then escapes by swimming through the hole in the windshield.

Danger Fact

French stunt driver Gil Delamare felt that a fast stop at high speed, using the handbrake to make the car skid, didn't require wearing a safety belt. The G-force threw him against the rear-view mirror, which resulted in his death from a fractured skull.

SPIELBERG'S STUNTS – INDIANA JONES

The names Craig Baxley, Bill Couch, and Charles Picerni are largely unknown by the general public, but without their expert skill *Dick Tracy*, *Ghostbusters*, and *Die Hard II* would have lacked the fights, falls, crashes, and thrills that make them the exciting films they are. These people are stunt coordinators, and their job is to supervise and interconnect all the scenes of action in an action film.

Simulated machine gun fire livens up this chase in *Raiders of the Lost Ark*.

A horse transfer stunt in *Raiders of the Lost Ark*.

One of the greatest screen action sequences was the chase in *Raiders of the Lost Ark*. The film's director, Steven Spielberg, wanted to make a film similar to the adventure serials he had been thrilled by as a boy. The script called for the film's hero to retrieve the stolen "ark" of the title from a small army of Nazi guards and vehicles. In a seven-minute sequence, Indiana Jones pursues the villains' convoy riding a horse over rocky terrain and does a transfer to the truck containing the ark. By the end of the sequence, he has single-handedly gotten rid of thirteen fully-armed soldiers, a military half-track with a mounted machine gun, a motorcycle combination, and a Mercedes Benz open touring-car. He achieves all this while never allowing the truck or its contents to get out of his control.

The scene was so complicated that *two* stunt coordinators – American Glenn Randell and Peter Diamond from Britain – are credited with making it a reality. They assembled a stunt team that was truly international; American, British, and European stunt performers and residents of Tunisia – where the film was made – worked alongside each other. Before filming began, the director had the sequence storyboarded. This means having it drawn as a comic-strip and following the strip shot-by-shot. Shooting began with the stunt team doubling for the principal actors. No stars in motion pictures ever do all their own stunts. This is because if a leading actor or actress is injured and forced to take time off it will cost a minimum of $100,000 a day to postpone work until he or she has recovered. Therefore, a stunt double stands by at all times, just in case.

Harrison Ford doing his own stunting in a fire sequence in *Raiders of the Lost Ark*.

Terry Leonard doubles for Harrison Ford in the famous chase scene in *Raiders of the Lost Ark*.

Terry Leonard did the bulk of the stunting for Harrison Ford, who played Indiana Jones. Leonard is an experienced horseman and noted for his work with vehicles – he was later to drive a Volkswagen over a waterfall in *Romancing the Stone*. He was, therefore, well qualified to perform all the action shots, including being dragged at high speed under the German army truck. However, a similar stunt on *The Legend of the Lone Ranger* had resulted in the wheels of a stagecoach passing over him and severely injuring his legs. This was his first time back at work. He was attempting the same stunt but under a heavier vehicle going considerably faster. A mistake this time could be fatal, so members of the cast and crew were understandably concerned. Thanks to the joint efforts of the coordinators, the stunt was completed without mishap. In fact, the safety precautions worked out so well that Harrison Ford was able to perform much more of the action than was originally planned for him.

It is a tribute to the ingenuity and attention to detail of the stunt coordinator and performers that the producers of the second and third Indiana Jones films – *The Temple of Doom* and *The Last Crusade* – can boast that no injuries to either cast or crew occurred. The work of stunt performers has played a large part in the excitement, enjoyment, and entertainment of films like these. Long may stunt men and women continue to thrill us. . . .

GLOSSARY

Action   The signal a film director gives for filming to begin.

Aerobatics   Spectacular or dangerous moves, such as loops or rolls, performed by aircraft.

Air bag   An inflatable plastic container used for high falls.

Air ram   A hinged board used to throw a stunt performer backward or forward. It works on compressed air.

Box rig   A high fall rig made up of cardboard cartons.

Descender wire   An attachment used for controlled high falls.

Doubles   Stunt performers who substitute for the main actors and actresses in dangerous scenes.

Drag leather   A device used by a stunt rider for being dragged by a horse.

Extras   Actors and actresses who feature in crowd scenes in a film. They do not have speaking parts.

Falling horse   A horse trained to fall on command.

G-force   The force of gravity increasing as an object moves faster.

Gag   Another term for stunt.

High fall rig   Apparatus used to cushion a stunt performer in the execution of a high fall. It is also known as a catcher.

Horse fall   A riding stunt in which the horse and rider fall over.

Jerk harness   A wire-assisted device that pulls a stunt performer over backward. It is also used to pull a rider from a horse.

"L" stirrup   An open-sided stirrup used as a safety aid when taking a saddle fall or making a transfer from a moving horse.

Music hall   A type of variety entertainment consisting of songs and jokes. Also called vaudeville.

Pad up   To put padding on the body to avoid bruising.

Racing broadside   Sliding a vehicle sideways.

Rollbar   A safety device in a car that prevents the roof from caving in on the driver.

Rollover   A stunt causing a car to turn over completely one or more times.

Saddle fall   A fall from a moving horse.

Second unit director   A person who directs action sequences and scenes using stunt doubles. He or she is usually an ex-stunt performer.

Sleight of hand   Skill used in performing conjuring tricks.

Somersault jacket   A leather vest with a hook and wire attachment used by stunt riders to assist in a back flip from a galloping horse.

Special effects   Techniques used to produce film sequences that cannot be filmed normally.

Sprung box rig   Cardboard cartons and mattresses mounted on a base of springy wooden planks resting on car inner tubes.

Stunt coordinator   A person responsible for setting up scenes of action and hiring stunt personnel for a film.

Take   A scene that the director is satisfied has been filmed successfully.

Trip wires   Wires attached to the legs of a galloping horse that cause the animal to fall over against its will. These are now illegal.

Whiplash   Injury to the neck caused by the head snapping back in a car crash.

INDEX

The numbers in **bold** refer to captions.

Airplane stunts 4, 9

Back to the Future III 18
Ben Hur 18
Body padding 10, **18**, 24
Bullitt 21

Canutt, Yakima 17-19
Car stunts 4, 7, 8, **11**, 21-5, 27, 29
Catchers (high fall rigs) 12, 13
Circus acrobats 7
Conan the Barbarian 18
Crash pads 13

Dances with Wolves 18
Days of Thunder 4
Death Sport 11
Descender wires 14, 15
Diamonds Are Forever 22
Dick Tracy 26
Die Hard II 26
Directors 6, 10

Early stunts 6-7, 8, 13, 19, 23
Earthquake 9
Explosives 4, 14, 15, 24

Falls 4, 6, **8**, 9, 10, 11, 12-14, 18, 26
Fire stunts 10, 14, **17**, **23**, **28**
Ford, Harrison **20**, **28**, 29

Ghostbusters 26
Glory 4

Highlander 4
Home Alone 4

Indiana Jones 26-9
  Last Crusade, The **20**, 29
  Raiders of the Lost Ark **26**, 27, **28**, **29**
  Temple of Doom, The **13**, 29

Jerk harness 15

Lethal Weapon **12**
License to Kill **4**
Lloyd, Harold **6**
Love Bug, The 22

Man with the Golden Gun, The 22, 23
McQueen, Steve 21
Moore, Roger 14

Police Academy 4

Redford, Robert 22
Robin Hood 4
Romancing the Stone 29

Schwarzenegger, Arnold **5**
Smokey & the Bandit 22
Smokey & the Bandit II 23
Special effects 14
Spielberg, Steven 26-9
Spy Who Loved Me, The 22

Stunt coordinators 14, 26, 29
Stunt riding 7, 9, 17-20, **27**
Stunt women 8-11
Superman 14

Top Gun 4

View to a Kill, A 22

Westerns 17

Young Guns II 18